YOUR PERSONAL GRIEF RECOVERY POCKETBOOK

Finding Light in the Darkness

The Perfect Companion For Those Journeying Through Grief

KATE L MORFOOT

To all those who have loved and lost.

Copyright ©2024 Kate Morfoot

All rights reserved. No part of this publication may be reproduced, distributed or transmitted in any form or by any means, including photocopying, recording, or other electronic or mechanical methods, without the prior written permission of the publisher, except in the case of brief quotations embodied in critical reviews and certain other non-commercial use permitted by copyright law.

TABLE OF CONTENTS

A Note From The Author 5

Introduction 6

Part One: Loss, The Curve Ball 8

Part Two: The stages of grief experienced and explained 12

Part Three: Coping Strategies 15

Part Four: The Journey Towards Healing 19

Part Five: Moving Forward 22

Part Six: Helplines for grief support 24

A Note From The Author

'Finding Light in the Darkness' is your personal grief recovery pocketbook, the perfect companion for anyone journeying through grief.

Let this book be your source of comfort, guidance, and hope as you navigate the path toward healing and renewal.

In times of loss and sorrow, finding solace can seem impossible. 'Finding Light in the Darkness' is here to guide you through the challenging journey of grief with compassion and understanding.

This compact yet comprehensive guide offers practical advice, heartfelt reflections, and supportive exercises to help you navigate the complexities of grief and begin your journey toward healing. Whether you're experiencing the loss of a loved one, a relationship, or a significant life change, this pocketbook is your companion in grief recovery, offering comfort and guidance whenever you need it most.

In this guide, you'll discover:

- Insights into the grieving process and common experiences.

- Strategies for coping with emotions like sadness, anger, and guilt.

- Tools for honouring your loved one's memory and finding meaning in your loss.

- Self-care practices to nurture your physical, emotional, and spiritual well-being.

- Guidance for navigating life transitions and rebuilding a sense of purpose.

- Inspirational quotes to uplift your spirits along the way.

Introduction

Grief is an intensely personal experience, and there's no universal way to navigate it.

Memories become both a source of solace and a source of pain in the wake of loss, casting long shadows over our hearts as we grapple with the bittersweet beauty of remembrance.

Heartache can surge through you unexpectedly, like turbulent ocean waves that crash over you without warning. Grief is a profound and enduring experience, it's likely that you will carry your sorrow with you for a long time, perhaps even forever.

However, the way you manage and cope with that grief can change over time, helping you to navigate life more effectively. Though it may feel as if you've been torn apart, through healing and support, you can find ways to feel whole again.

Grief is a multifaceted and deeply personal experience that can arise from a wide range of losses. It isn't limited to the death of a loved one; it encompasses any significant change or loss that impacts our lives profoundly.

Each type of grief has its own unique challenges and emotional responses. It's important to recognise that all these experiences are valid forms of grief and deserve compassion and understanding. Seeking support, whether through friends, family, or professional counselling, can be a crucial part of the healing process.

Has it ever amazed you how some people seem 'very good' at coping with grief. I have often wondered what makes these individuals appear so emotionally strong. But are they really?

On the other hand, many people struggle profoundly and cannot come to terms with their loss. They go through the various cycles of grief but do not ever seem to heal from it.

Grief thrusts us into the unknown, forcing us to confront the uncertainties of life and certainty of death. Grief is how we are forced to confront our deepest fears and darkest doubts, finding strength in the resilience of the human spirit and the bonds that endure even in the face of loss.

The transformative power of grief, the seeds of growth that lie hidden amidst the rubble of sorrow, and the possibility of finding hope in the most unexpected places is the journey of grief.

> "So it's true, when all is said and done, grief is the price we pay for love."
> *E.A. Bucchianeri, Brushstrokes of a Gadfly*

Part One: Loss, The Curve Ball

You didn't see that coming. The news of the sudden death of a loved one or a pet can invoke feelings of shock, sickness, and disbelief. The curve ball hits, and life is turned upside down. Suddenly, you are dealing with the aftereffects and the enormity of the news, and the unknown impact on how it's going to affect you, your life, and those around you.

Fear and anxiety can take hold, and you can't see the wood from the trees. Each day feels numb until the severity of the situation starts to unfold. How to cope with life never being the same again?

Loss is a profoundly personal and transformative experience, often striking without warning and leaving a trail of emotional turmoil. The initial shock can be paralyzing, making it difficult to process the reality of what has happened. This disorientation can permeate all aspects of life, leaving you struggling to comprehend the magnitude of the change.

In the immediate aftermath, feelings of fear and anxiety are common. These emotions stem from the uncertainty of how this loss will reshape your world. The future, once predictable, now feels precarious and unknown. The numbness you feel is a natural defence mechanism, giving you a temporary reprieve from the full force of your grief.

To navigate this tumultuous period, it's crucial to acknowledge your emotions and give yourself permission to grieve. There is no "right" way to mourn; each person's journey is unique. Allow yourself to feel the pain, confusion, and sadness. Bottling up these emotions can lead to prolonged suffering and can impede the healing process.

Lean on your support system. Friends, family, and loved ones can provide comfort and companionship during this difficult time. Don't hesitate to reach out and share your feelings with those you trust. Sometimes, talking about your loss can help you process it and begin to understand its impact on your life.

Consider seeking professional help. Therapists and counsellors are trained to help individuals cope with grief and can offer strategies to manage your emotions. Support groups can also be beneficial, providing a space to connect with others who are experiencing similar losses.

As you move through your grief, try to find small ways to honour the memory of your loved one or pet. This could be through a memorial service, creating a photo album, or simply taking time each day to reflect on happy memories. These acts of remembrance can help you feel connected to what you've lost and provide a sense of continuity.

Understand that healing is a gradual process. There will be days when the pain feels overwhelming and others when you can see glimpses of hope. Be patient with yourself and allow time to heal your wounds. Life may never be the same again, but with time and support, you can find a new normal and continue to cherish the memories of what you've lost.

In summary, the sudden loss of a loved one or a pet is a profound shock that can leave you feeling disoriented and numb. By acknowledging your emotions, seeking support, and finding ways to honour your loss, you can begin to navigate this challenging period and move towards healing.

"The weird, weird thing about devastating loss is that life actually goes on. When you're faced with a tragedy, a loss so huge that you have no idea how you can live through it, somehow, the world keeps turning, the seconds keep ticking."
James Patterson, Angel

The inevitable loss that still hurts

Even when you anticipate the end of something significant—a loved one, a pet, a relationship, a job, or even children moving out—the actual moment it happens can still feel overwhelming. The void it leaves behind can bring feelings of emptiness and loneliness, making it hard to fill that space. It often takes time to come to terms with the loss before you can begin to rediscover happiness.

Inner grief

For many people it's hard to grieve. Grieving can be challenging for many individuals. Some may only realize years later that what they experienced was indeed grief, which went unrecognized or unaddressed at the time. Whether mourning the loss of a loved one, the end of a relationship or job, or the pain of miscarriage, internal grief can often remain hidden. Adopting the "stiff upper lip" mentality or avoiding the topic due to societal taboos or a desire not to inconvenience others can lead to the burial of one's grief. Ultimately, choosing to soldier on without expressing or processing emotions may result in the suppression of grief, complicating its resolution.

Whether it's grieving through death an end of a relationship, job or miscarriage, whatever it is, sometimes, inner grief can be buried. Taking the 'stiff upper lip' approach or whether it's a taboo subject or not wanting to cause a fuss, just best to carry on without causing concern from others, can ultimately cause your grief to be buried.

Exploring the Depths of Inner Grief

The sense of loss manifests in various ways – the loss of innocence in childhood or the devastating loss of a loved one through violence or tragedy.

Unaddressed grief can seep into mental well-being, erode relationships, and foster a downward spiral into despair. Signs such as increased substance use or a persistent sense of unhappiness might indicate unresolved grief and its accompanying symptoms.

Many individuals, in the immediate aftermath of loss, attempt to resume their daily routines, seemingly brushing aside the monumental impact of the event. However, this avoidance only postpones the inevitable confrontation with one of life's most heart-wrenching experiences.

Suppressing grief will inevitably resurface. Often, the need for proper grieving emerges later, sometimes years after the initial loss. It's crucial to recognize and address grief, allowing for healing and eventual peace.

Part Two: The stages of grief experienced and explained

Grief can be very debilitating, affecting every aspect of your life.

You may experience a lack of appetite, change in sleeping patters, concentration, weaker immune system, panic attacks and generally unhappiness.

The stages of grief may help you to understand the processes that you are going through and be helpful for those around to support you.

Anger | Anxiety | Depression | Disbelief | Fear | Guilt | Loneliness | Suicidal Thoughts | Worry |

Each of these stages, for which some or all may be experienced at different stages in the grieving process are normal and will pass. It is important to realise that you are human and as humans we feel extreme anguish in these intense moments of grief.

Anger and anxiety can take over, leading to moments, days or months of depression. The severity of your anxiety can be put into perspective. With time and support these feelings can be overcome.

The stages of grief, often referred to as the "five stages of grief," were first introduced by Elisabeth Kübler-Ross in her 1969 book "On Death and Dying." These stages represent the range of emotions that people experience when dealing with loss. While originally applied to terminally ill patients, they have been widely adopted to describe the grieving process more generally. The stages are not necessarily experienced in order, and individuals may move back and forth between stages or experience them differently.

Stages of Grief: Characteristics and Examples

1. Denial

- Characteristics: Shock, disbelief, and numbness. A person may have trouble accepting the reality of the loss.

- Example: "This can't be happening. There must be some mistake."

2. Anger

- Characteristics: Frustration, rage, and irritation. This anger can be directed at oneself, others, or the situation.

- Example: "Why is this happening to me? It's not fair."

3. Bargaining

- Characteristics: Attempting to make deals or negotiate with a higher power or within oneself to postpone or mitigate the loss.

- Example: "If I could just have more time, I promise I'll change."

4. Depression

- Characteristics: Deep sadness, regret, and hopelessness. This stage involves mourning the loss and recognizing its impact.

- Example: "I can't go on without them. Everything is so overwhelming."

5. Acceptance

- Characteristics: Coming to terms with the reality of the loss. This doesn't mean being "okay" with it but finding a way to live with it.

- Example: "I have to move on and adjust to this new reality."

Additional Insights

- Non-linear Process: People do not necessarily experience these stages in a linear order. It's common to revisit stages multiple times or experience multiple stages simultaneously.

- Individual Variation: Each person's grief journey is unique. Cultural, social, personal, and situational factors can all influence how someone grieves.

- Beyond Five Stages: Some models of grief include additional stages, such as shock before denial or finding meaning after acceptance.

- Other Models: There are other theories and models of grief, such as William Worden's "Tasks of Mourning" or Therese Rando's "Six Rs."

Understanding these stages can help individuals recognize their feelings and seek appropriate support during the grieving process. It's also essential to remember that there is no "right" way to grieve, and everyone's experience is valid.

Part Three: Coping Strategies

Mornings and evenings can be the most anxious times when dealing with grief. As you process your thoughts, these times can also be the loneliest. Your grief can be the last thing you think about at night and the first thing you think about in the morning.

Here are some examples of useful coping strategies:-

Mornings

- Wake up to music, the radio or the TV
- Get up straightway to take a hot shower or bath
- Journal how you feel each morning and what your plans are for the day ahead
- If living alone- make a phone call and have some human contact
- Spend at least 20 minutes each morning outside
- Take each day as it comes

Anytime

- Take time out to grieve, wail, scream if you need to

Evenings

- Talk to a friend, family member
- Journal how you felt during the day, what was good, bad or indifferent
- Take a hot shower or bath before bed and light a candle
- Eat something delicious- Be kind to yourself – self-care is important
- Avoid watching doom or gloom TV
- Ensure your bedroom is ready for a good night's sleep

Coping with grief can be a profoundly personal experience, but there are several strategies that can help individuals navigate through their sorrow. Here are some effective coping mechanisms:

Emotional Expression and Support

1. **Talk About Your Feelings:** Share your emotions with friends, family, or a therapist. Talking can help process the grief.

2. **Join Support Groups:** Connecting with others who are experiencing similar losses can provide comfort and understanding.

Self-Care

3. **Maintain a Routine:** Keeping a regular schedule can provide a sense of normalcy.

4. **Exercise:** Physical activity can improve mood and reduce stress.

5. **Eat Healthily:** Proper nutrition supports overall well-being.

6. **Rest:** Ensure you get enough sleep to help your body cope with stress.

Mindfulness and Relaxation

7. **Practice Mindfulness or Meditation:** These techniques can help you stay grounded and manage overwhelming emotions.

8. **Engage in Hobbies:** Pursue activities you enjoy providing temporary distraction and a sense of fulfilment.

Creative Outlets

9. **Express Through Art:** Writing, painting, or other creative activities can be therapeutic.

10. Keep a Journal: Documenting your thoughts and feelings can provide an outlet for your emotions.

Commemoration

11. Create Rituals or Memorials: Honouring the memory of a loved one through rituals or creating a memorial can provide solace.

12. Celebrate Life or Achievements: Focus on positive memories and celebrate the life lived or achievements fulfilled.

Professional Help

13. Seek Therapy: A professional therapist can offer coping strategies and a safe space to explore your grief.

14. Consider Medication: In some cases, medication might be necessary to manage severe symptoms of grief or depression (consult a healthcare provider).

Social Connections

15. Stay Connected: Maintain relationships with friends and family, even if it's just through brief interactions.

Acceptance and Patience

16. Allow Yourself to Grieve: Accept that grieving is a necessary process and that it takes time.

17. Be Patient: Understand that healing is gradual and that it's okay to have good and bad days.

Educational Resources

18. Read About Grief: Books and articles on grief can provide insights and strategies.

19. Online Resources: Websites and forums can offer additional support and information.

Giving Back

20. Volunteer: Helping others can provide a sense of purpose and can be a way to honour a loved one's memory.

Spiritual Practices

21. Engage in Spiritual Activities: If you have spiritual beliefs, activities such as prayer, meditation, or attending services can provide comfort.

Practical Adjustments

22. Set Small Goals: Break tasks into manageable pieces to avoid feeling overwhelmed.

23. Be Kind to Yourself: Recognize that it's okay to not be okay and that self-compassion is crucial.

Grieving is a unique experience for each person, and it's important to find the strategies that work best for you.

Part Four: The Journey Towards Healing

"No one ever told me that grief felt so like fear." C.S. Lewis

Grief is a journey without a defined endpoint. While you may carry it with you always, the intensity and the way it affects you can evolve. Support from others, self-care, and finding personal meaning can help you navigate life more effectively. Although you may feel broken, healing and support can guide you toward a sense of wholeness once more.

Remember, grief is a testament to the love and connection you had with the person or pet you've lost. It's a natural response to loss and finding your own way through it is a deeply personal and transformative process.

Think about you and your needs for each moment of each stage of the grieving process.

Health

Grief takes a toll on your health and mental health. Lack of sleep and appetite will play havoc with your immune system, making you more susceptible to illness. You may have noticed over the past months, eating badly and drinking more alcohol has played a bigger role.

Regaining Energy- Healing time is healing your mind and your body

- Healthy meal planning making sure you have three meals a day
- Take some vitamin supplements for an immune boost
- Drink kefir and kombucha to improve your gut health
- Check your alcohol units, decrease or cut out alcohol
- Cut down or give up smoking / drugs
- Get a health check up
- Assess medication
- Walking or exercise at least 20 minutes a day outside

Out of your Comfort Zone

- Reverse your routine, do different and feel different
- Dare to dream, is there something you want to do?
- Plan a trip to somewhere you've always wanted to go
- Call a friend that you haven't spoken to in months
- Join a group or club that interests you
- Take up a new hobby or start the one you left
- Take up a volunteering role
- Find a new job

Laugh again

- Don't feel guilty about laughing or having fun
- Watch funny YouTube or Instagram videos
- Watch feel good movies
- Spend time with friends and family who you enjoy being with
- Laugh about the old times

Self Esteem

- Have a daily routine that makes you feel good! Shower, shave, use your perfume/aftershave, wear your best clothes, put on your makeup and do your hair
- You are what you eat; eat healthy food and enjoy three meals a day
- Exercise to make your endorphins fizz and feel better mentally and physically
- Pick up on friendships and plan for days out and days of the week and evenings that you find hard.
- Buy some indoor and outdoor plants
- Get some bird feeders and take time to watch nature

- If you find yourself alone, at a loose end, plan for movie night with good food, a hot bath and candle and get ready for the next day
- Try yoga, meditation or deep breathing exercises to relax
- Journal your days and recovery and look how far you've come

Part Five: Moving Forward

"Grief is in two parts. The first is loss. The second is the remaking of life."

Anne Roiphe

The journey through grief is not about "getting over" a loss but learning to move forward with it. It's about finding a new normal, where the pain of the loss does not overshadow the potential for happiness and fulfilment.

Healing from grief does not mean forgetting or negating the loss. It means learning to live with it in a way that allows for peace and joy to coexist with the memory of your loved one.

Set New Goals: Gradually begin to set personal and professional goals that excite and motivate you.

Celebrate Life: Honor the life of your loved one by living your life fully and embracing new opportunities.

Hold On to Hope: Trust that the intensity of grief will lessen over time, and a new chapter of your life will unfold, one where the memory of your loved one brings warmth rather than pain.

Grief is a testament to the depth of our love. Overcoming it is not about erasing the past but about integrating the experience into a richer, more compassionate understanding of life. It is a journey of resilience, and with each step, we move closer to healing and wholeness.

Healing from grief is a personal journey that takes time. Be patient with yourself, seek support when needed, and remember that it's okay to experience joy again. This pocketbook is here to provide hope and comfort as you navigate your path to recovery and ultimate happiness again in whatever shape or form.

> *"Only time and tears take away grief; that is what they are for."*
> Terry Pratchett, I Shall Wear Midnight

Part Six: Helplines for grief support

Seeking Support

Grieving can be an isolating experience, but it is important to remember that support is available. Connecting with others can provide comfort and perspective.

Lean on Loved Ones: Share your feelings with family and friends who understand your pain.

Join Support Groups: Being with others who are experiencing similar losses can provide a sense of community and understanding.

Professional Help: Therapists and counsellors can offer guidance and strategies for coping.

International Helplines

1. Crisis Text Line: Text HOME to 741741 (USA and Canada) for crisis counseling.

2. Samaritans: Call 116 123 (UK and Ireland) for emotional support.

3. Befrienders Worldwide: Visit [Befrienders.org](https://www.befrienders.org) for international support contacts.

United Kingdom:

1. Cruse Bereavement Care: Call 0808 808 1677 or visit [Cruse.org.uk](https://www.cruse.org.uk) for grief support.

2. Child Bereavement UK: Call 0800 02 888 40 for support after the death of a child or young person.

3. Nelson's Journey: Call 01603 431788 for children who have experienced the death of a significant person.

4. Winston's Wish: Call 08088 020 021 for support for grieving children and their families

5. YANA: Call 0300 323 0400 for support for mental health for those involved in agriculture affected by stress and depression / grieving over the loss of a loved one.

United States:

1. National Suicide Prevention Lifeline: Call 1-800-273-TALK (8255) or text HELLO to 741741 for emotional crisis support.

2. GriefShare: Visit [GriefShare.org] (https://www.griefshare.org) or call 1-800-395-5755 for group support and resources.

3. The Compassionate Friends: Call 1-877-969-0010 for grief support after the death of a child.

Canada:

1. Canadian Mental Health Association (CMHA): Visit [CMHA.ca] (https://cmha.ca) for resources and local support contacts.

2. Kids Help Phone: Call 1-800-668-6868 or text CONNECT to 686868 for support for children and youth.

Australia:

1. GriefLine: Call 1300 845 745 for grief support services.

2. Lifeline Australia: Call 13 11 14 for crisis support and suicide prevention.

New Zealand:

1. Skylight: Call 0800 299 100 for grief support services and resources.

2. Youthline: Call 0800 376 633 or text 234 for support for young people.

These helplines provide various forms of support, including counselling, emotional support, and resources for coping with grief.

Printed in Great Britain
by Amazon